At the Altar of Touch

Born in Beijing, Gavin Yuan Gao is a genderqueer, bilingual immigrant poet who grew up in Beijing and Brisbane. They hold a BA (magna cum laude) in English Literature and Creative Writing from The University of Michigan, Ann Arbor. They live in Brisbane and read poetry for *The Adroit Journal*. *At the Altar of Touch* is their first book.

THE ARTS QUEENSLAND THOMAS SHAPCOTT POETRY PRIZE SERIES

Lidija Cvetkovic *War Is Not the Season for Figs*
Jaya Savige *latecomers*
Nathan Shepherdson *Sweeping the Light Back into the Mirror*
Angela Gardner *Parts of Speech*
Sarah Holland-Batt *Aria*
Felicity Plunkett *Vanishing Point*
Rosanna Licari *An Absence of Saints*
Vlanes *Another Babylon*
Nicholas Powell *Water Mirrors*
Rachael Briggs *Free Logic*
David Stavanger *The Special*
Krissy Kneen *Eating My Grandmother: a grief cycle*
Stuart Barnes *Glasshouses*
Shastra Deo *The Agonist*
Rae White *Milk Teeth*
Anna Jacobson *Amnesia Findings*
Luke Best *Cadaver Dog*

Gavin **Yuan Gao**

At the Altar of Touch

UQP

First published 2022 by University of Queensland Press
PO Box 6042, St Lucia, Queensland 4067 Australia
Reprinted 2023

University of Queensland Press (UQP) acknowledges the Traditional Owners and their custodianship of the lands on which UQP operates. We pay our respects to their Ancestors and their descendants, who continue cultural and spiritual connections to Country. We recognise their valuable contributions to Australian and global society.

uqp.com.au
reception@uqp.com.au

Cover design by Sandy Cull, www.sandycull.com
Typeset in 11.5/15 pt Bembo Std by Post Pre-press Group, Brisbane
Printed in Australia by McPherson's Printing Group

Queensland Government

This project is supported by the Queensland Government through Arts Queensland.

Australian Government | Australia Council for the Arts

University of Queensland Press is assisted by the Australian Government through the Australia Council, its arts funding and advisory body.

A catalogue record for this book is available from the National Library of Australia

ISBN 978 0 7022 6334 7 (pbk)
ISBN 978 0 7022 6517 4 (epdf)

University of Queensland Press uses papers that are natural, renewable and recyclable products made from wood grown in well-managed forests and other controlled sources. The logging and manufacturing processes conform to the environmental regulations of the country of origin.

MIX
Paper | Supporting responsible forestry
FSC® C001695
FSC www.fsc.org

For my mother, Liping Yuan (1962–1999)

Contents

I Coup de grâce

II The Moon's Annotations

III Riverborne

IV At the Altar of Touch

V The Resurrection

I Coup de grâce

Self-Portrait as the Last Wounded Stag

I'm walking into the quickening blizzard
as if into a hunter's dream—

the flint arrow through my chest keener
than earthly desire. Wherever I went

teeth followed me, relentless as the shadow
of the doe-eyed boy I thought

I couldn't live without. Long ago, love
made all gestures of flowering

possible on earth. Now I'm tired of living
on the peripheries where the witch-hazels thicken

as inkblots & the light over the hill grows
more distant each year. Father, far

& reticent as you are, let me not be a memory
of blood & musk salting a wolf's breath.

Let me be antlers. Let me be lightning
branching jagged into sky. Let me be sky—

Coup de grâce

Think back to that autumn when
the month-long fever could've claimed
the frail light of your child-self, pure
enough to believe the end
of one life could be the finale of all
despairs. Then think of your father's
hands, work-wrecked & threadbare, cradling
the sallow gibbous moon of your face.
Later, when snow came too early
like a borrowed future, filling up window
boxes, deepening around the ankles
of your hunting boots, you'd gladly follow
that sweet trail of windfall apples to the crayoned
edge of childhood beyond the barbed wire fences
had your father not called to you
through the woods, through the twilight
prison-striped by the silver birches. Remember
how he carried the weight of the dead
in his shotgun, which he'd polished with a felt scrap
until the muzzle glinted like a slick
engagement ring around a solar eclipse.
He'd shown you how to shuck a bullet, how
to crack a life open through the centre
of its skull. But that was before the fever turned
your cheeks crescent. Before loss appeared
as real as the frost dulling the back
of his ungloved hand. Before you both saw

the last breath struggle to crest the snout
of that wounded fox, which, red as the windfall
apple, had dragged a trap-clamped leg all the way
from a badland in the far north,
where nothing would grow or come
to its rescue & every light was the feeble light
of diminishment. Your father pushed
the shotgun's darkening weight into your palms, saying
with his wind-worn eyes, *End its suffering, end it*
before it enters you & is yours forever, as if mercy
were a gift, relentless as the animal will to live,
though all you could think of was a body so still
that it became a kind of listening, a listening so complete
it required your bones to sing to it, until you forgot
the winter of your own body, how you pulled
the trigger towards the white wreath of your breath,
felt a shudder—how the trees leaned to claim the silence
of that temporal space & finally, sated, leaned back again.

Luna Moth

The day they returned your ashes
in a marble urn, I saw it land
on the ballet shoes you'd left behind.

A winged whisper planted right
at the centre of summer, almost too delicate
for the season—I lifted it up,

its plumed thorax glowing in
the moon-striped dark. Its wings
were sheer, gossamer & lightning on the tips

of the satin slippers, stippled pink
from your training years—you who exacted
from yourself such discipline,

cartography-precise in each step: bold
leaps, controlled pirouettes, tracing
the stage with your chafed toe.

Grandma rescued these shoes from the fire
that chewed your bones. She'd washed them
by hand after each performance, scrubbing

them with soapsuds even on days when
the snow outside barricaded the pine wood door
of your single-roomed home.

She'd rinsed her years in the frigid pool
of the cement basin. Calluses had consecrated
her palms, so when the cremating flames

bit her hand she didn't flinch.
Love had turned her skin to grooved bark,
a labour-hardened body the elements

could no longer harm: unburnt, undrowned.
Yet she wept that night seeing the green spirit
manifest itself on the windowsill.

The moth alighted on the blemished fabric,
a messenger guided into our world. Mother,
do you dance barefoot on the other side?

Did you send it here? —this moonlight-gilded
ancient shield, this little pale-green mask that,
if you put it on, death would never find you.

Or was it you, shaking the soot from your body,
who changed shape & came back to the light we had
shared? One child, two women at a table.

I tried to grasp the soothing nocturne of its
speech—this spirit of you. *Stay with us
a little longer*, I pleaded in human language.

Patient pilot of the earthly hours, rest
your wings against my palms.
I never doubted your faithfulness.

I've always known that the soul's
colour, like spring, is the green
of budding foliage.

The Afterlife

after her funeral, my mother lives forever
in the bricked-up chamber
of my father's camera,   negative
& undeveloped.   body as ink traced on silver
lamina.   body as final verdict against
the fiction of decay.   never mind my father
locking heaven away in a strongbox.
never mind grief licking his heart
down to a pale pearl.   I imagine the frames
each one   a painstakingly planked dove house
from which my mother stares out, her face a lighthouse
on the island of memory   around which
her unspent years   hover in ghost orbs.   somewhere
along the wound-up strip of dark windows, she lies
spread-eagled on a frozen lake   while the shadow
of her future self swims past her under ice
as a grin makes her face blossom   into light.
oh mama dove   snow angel
tell me   this isn't the life
you've always   wanted.

1999, or The Year of Mulberry

The year the shadow grew ravenous
        & made a kingdom of your bones

The year I finally mastered the art
        of bike riding without training wheels

The year I was told the mulberry tree you
        & Dad had planted in front of our home
                wouldn't live past June

The year the sea rose & for three weeks
                all the lambs in my dreams had coats
        matted with salt flakes

The year of short-lived winter, though it snowed
                for months in our hearts as we gathered
        around your hospital bed

The year a rare asteroid chalking its way
                across our galaxy was named
        after a Golden Age starlet
who was immortalised for her love
                                of the spotlight

The year that stood like a wrought-iron gate
        between the new millennium & the public
                cemetery where Dad would've laid

you to rest, where even in death
                    you'd be self-effacing—your head
          a tufted pillow for the milkweeds
                                        to sleep & dream on

The year the mulberry lived, whose
          chain-mail fruits Dad & I spent a whole
afternoon collecting in a bamboo basket
                    but neither of us wanted to eat

The year I lost my treasured bike but didn't tell the sea

The year I allowed myself
          to miss you & only told the mulberry
as I stroked its dry bark. A loose wind
                    knuckled its mottled leaves
          freckling my cheeks with the sun's warm coins

as if it was the only one who'd grasped
          what I didn't say
                    couldn't say (for loss was still the coppice
that lay beyond the border
          of my young tongue)   & grieved with me

Skein Song

Next time, fight back. By all means, break
their necks, my grandma said that night
as she set aside her needlework to rub
ointment on my black eye

which swelled up with pride like a swamp, *Show*
them what you're made of. Unlike most
Chinese grandparents, she was no evangelist
for cosmic harmony or silent
suffering. The fugitive of thorns

& lightning, she was secret knowledge
polished to a stealthy gleam
by sirens & famine. She was the napalm-grazed

forest at the edge of which
a girl once had her dress peeled off
by a pack of soldiers, whose wolf-eyes drank
from her mercilessly as they groped
the small pale fruits of her breasts

while the shrapnel went on blooming
around her. & how I'm reminded
that the strongest rope
I've ever held is braided from
the hair of the women I know. Women

who'd barred dragons & witches
from my dreams with their soothing voices. Who,
when told not to scream by the police, raised
their heads in the slanting rain
and stamped the sky with their hearty cries.

The night flowed slow
as my grandma wove
the warp & weft of time. She pushed
her needle through a handkerchief
the way a soprano threads a tremolo
through the fabric of her heart & out sprang tiger

lilies crimson as the doomsday sun. Her face
in the lamplight crude & wrinkled
like the last oak tree stump
on the riverbank. Each furrow

a quiet hum of simple flesh.

Distant Hills

After our strenuous lovemaking, the emperor
sleeps beside me the way his sword sleeps
as a silver hunger in its engraved sheath.

I watch his breath unfold in the dark into
a cut-glass peony, his body beautiful
as a wind-distilled cloud is beautiful—stalled

briefly by the sorrow of the doves' call.
Tomorrow, he will ride east & the jade-green
mountains flanking the battlefield will retreat

farther into his eyes. He who commanded
my flesh to swell with the thrill of a finely
plucked zither. He who, rising, once severed

the silken sail of his own embroidered sleeve
so as not to wake me. Always a sullen tribe,
the maples have stippled the airy dominion of

the courtyard with their passionless fires
so that tonight, whatever sadness I'm wounded by
can be revised into soft, wordless sighs.

& he will go on sleeping beside me as if blameless;
as if dawn—arriving with its quiver
of gold-leafed arrows—holds no promise of blood:

his lips still glazed with the sweetness of a song,
his areolae hardened by the autumn chill into
small moonlit graves. Except there is no moon

nor wind or dawn. Only distant hills, pale as mounds
of salt, against whose stoic shadows
my silence falls without witness.

Bait: A Queer Myth

When history looks back, I want to be
remembered as the small red fox
who once set a trap for the hunter.

Royal with want, I leapt & flickered
like a fever all winter as he followed me
into the hidden part of the myth.

This, of course, was the twentieth year
of my frayed breath. The sky, obscured
by the clouds' desire, bore down on us

like a swollen eyelid. I let him catch me, felt
his untethered strength shifting
inside my softness with the patience

of snow, our bodies rippling towards clarity
as moonlight swallowed our loud flesh.
His exhaustion afterwards, his cold

formality—how salt gleamed across
our shadows on the bare ground. I watched
him struggle to pull on his boots. Watched him

get up & disappear into the rest of the year.
I can still taste the wind from the back
of his throat. I think I always will.

Edifice

For twenty years, I've been breaking my jaw on the laws
in my father's house, as large & hard-shelled

as his sclerotic heart, until my teeth are dethroned
from their perches and turn the colour of early dusk.

I never ask my blood *Why* when I see it—a bright-red
treacherous smear on the white wall—afraid

it'd be the wrong question to ask. But isn't any kind of
questioning a sacrilege in this house, every desire of mine

dangerous & obscene? My father regrets my birth, his mouth
birthing the verdict of guilty against everything I hold dear.

Always, concrete & cinderblocks meet my bones when I try
to teach my body to be tender. Always, I pledge

& press my mouth to the light I've invited in through
the window before realising it's the wrong kind of light (*Fire!*

Fire!) & it slices through skin like a scalpel. I shelter
every lovable thing under the hot coal of my tongue—the navel

of another boy coiled like a serpent, asleep, his luscious
nipple the fruit I was forbidden to eat—but nothing

stays still and it aches the way the sky aches on a clear day
for rain. My father says the house itself

is an answer, a revelation that cracks clear in broad
daylight like lightning through a willow. But why is it

that I still wake up every morning with a monolith
tethered to my diaphragm, my breathing tied

to the foundation of this edifice? I see my father's sword
sharp & agleam on his mantle, daring not to imagine

what he has severed with it, & what he hasn't.

For the Man on the Bus Who Told Me to Go Back to Where I Came From

There are darker continents than you could dream
where children with skin only a shade
lighter than the brown earth
cup their hands around their mouths & wake

the mountains with their brazen lungs, while
the tea field gleams & echoes
with the name of every leaf & sparrow. For each birdsong

a barnhouse, a boathouse. Bales of hay
beside which our mother has placed,
with care, ears of maize
rows of gold
teeth swaddled in soft green, & a stand

of willows to which our grandfather had tied
the long years of his servitude, laying
down his storied life like an ox
relieved of the weight of the iron plough.

Where I come from, we dig & sow
until the dirt eats away the lines
in our palms. We write our lineage with spades
solemnly in the book of the good turf.

You do not know the place I come from.

Where I come from, we bathe
in the river's blazing dusk, wash the day
off of our wrists & faces
then each emerges
unburnt as a young phoenix.

Do not claim
to know where we come from.

Our language is the rain
pattering against rooftops
when the field's fire won't stop.

We whisper tender shoots
into the spring soil
and bury our roots so deep
no axe will cut them loose.

II The Moon's Annotations

Abing Addresses the Shadow of the Camphor Tree

Tonight, Brother, there'll be no secrets
between us. No easy dreams to

sing this life away. I shall speak to you
as a cinched echo to the green ghost

of a ripple, as one spurned exile to another.
All day, the bow of my erhu burned sweetly

across the twin strings & made them sigh
like the fishing line my father cast out

years ago, cleaving the summer air with a clean
swoosh to hook the mouth of a silver trout

& isn't all music, in essence, a hunger—the kind
that polishes the spirit to a lush spark

like a match scratched into light? I've been told
that I house a cold soul. *Let me guide you*

to Him, a missionary once said to me
in his efficient Chinese, his voice furred

with the lure of pity, *Let the Lord lift you*
into His light. But I've always loved

darkness—even before my eyes were silenced
—as darkness has always loved me, guarding me

at night in her clumsy mothering. Forgive
me, Brother. Memory numbs my mouth

like this jar of plum wine. The wind is full
of apologies though it has a wicked tongue. Listen

as it turns a phrase now, erasing the moon's
annotations on the river's darkening margin.

Abing Speaks to the Moon about the Loss of His Vision

Cast into the streets, I curse
this skin-tight hour of slumber
& waking. Curse this blight that evicted

your light from the guesthouses
of my eyes. All winter, I petitioned the sky
to revoke its decree of heavy snow,

prayed for the boiling tide in my lungs
to ebb—so the steel strings between
my fingers could speak in worship

of the fleeting quiet before each dawn
with the faith & fluency of a rooster.
Instead, fever licked my vision bone-clean,

whittled my body down to such lightness
I wore it through the day like a whispered
confession. But even in such loss

there's a sacredness. A hymn. As darkness
rises like steam behind my eyes, my hearing
brightens into ice: I hear summer

moult into autumn, persimmons
untethered from stalwart branches
thudding like bells of flesh.

I hear the precise, surgical knife
of each pitying sigh as a coin glides
like a cold note along the chipped edge

of my china bowl, coming to rest
at its centre the way a shiver lands in the small
of my back when the wind trespasses.

Faithful listener in the tree. Let me
lay down this vagrant life at your feet
& run a palm along the slender neck

of my erhu. Feel the strings eager
to unstitch the stillness as my heart
turns from barrenness to praise.

Abing Prays to the Ghost of His Seamstress Mother

All night, I hear you breathing at the window:
the soul of rain struck wide awake
                                        stitches distance
into new skeins of lilac blooms, each spray
a precarious skiff lurching on waves
of the bough's trembling that shyly
transmits news of a dim perfume.

Once, you too flowered in a dew
-bright season. When you flowered no more,
I staggered, a child of four, in the icy light
of your leaving & cried after your ash.
                                        Ashen the colour
of my malnourished cheek mirrored
in the frozen creek's ceaseless calm. Ashen
the morning sky thick with goosedown drift, its scrim
unfurled above the funeral procession
funnelled towards your burial hour.

All night, I hear you breathing at the window
as if you have not finished
with living: limbs of rain
                                        fracturing over
& over again upon the stony landscape

as you lay love's table over the water
-darkened skull of every rock, acquitting
no shadow, diminishing no loss.

                                        Mother, no hymn
will flood through me tonight as I lie
trembling with shame. I have no frankincense
to light for you. Only the muck-clouded
ponds of my eyes that answer to darkness
& darkness alone. But, for you, I will light them
with the salt welling from deep within. For you
my blindness burns a path
across the pathless world.

One Time, My Father, Crying, Drove into the Dusk

The tears he'd tried to rein back wrestled
his eyes. Waves of brightness. Wings

without bodies quivering in the cage
of his skull. Then he let it out

the way he'd surrendered Mum's ashes
to the sea's rough guardianship

weeks before—tentative palmfuls at first
then the whole silver urn—while the dusk

was the gold-teethed jaws of God
into which my father's beat-up Chevrolet

hurtled like a bruised fist until
there was no dusk or road at all.

Those were the days when tear
was the only unit in which love

was measured carefully against grief.
Private to a fault, my father dug

so deeply to bury his wounds
it seemed that, even in the keen eyes

of our kith & kin, he did not love her.
But he did. In his slow, watchful way,

recalling the rain's cellophane fingers
dimpling the water in our bird bath,

the scent of persimmons ripening
to a boyish blush in a wicker basket

balanced on the window ledge,
& my mother—the hostess,

the smiling goddess lost on earth
in a human kitchen—kneading her joy

into the sourdough, kneading her
hums & laughter into the hearts

around the table until her voice
hung clear & distinct in my head

as an icicle in a summer town. That
was a lifetime ago. After the funeral,

my father stood in the emptiness
of the same kitchen: everywhere he turned,

light refused to veil her absence. If only
he knew how to dissolve, how to seep

into the ocean like the shadow of an albatross
& teach her bones to unwilt. If only

he could've willed his eyes to a brief drought
before his focus melted away,

before his hands softened their grip
on the steering wheel as the car dove

straight into the roadside crops.
A trail of smoke rose from the engine

like the husky voice of the devil
crooning his weary blues on the car radio.

My father climbed out from the wreck,
shouldering his way through the cornstalks

in a daze. He licked the wind off his lips—
its taste brackish as loss. Still,

the future fanned out before him like
the wind-combed field, awaiting him

with the patience of a still sea
ever prepared to claim the dead

from the arms of the living.
Over the blackening field

the moon bloomed, elegant & cruel
as a harvest of ivory.

He lifted his hands through the dark
to cup its face. For a moment,

the moon was his.

Glass City Aubade

Nights shipwrecked / in nameless wanting

The city a floating glass
garden / to be lost in

Banished from the blinked-out streets / we put
our dollar-store faith / in the claw machine

Wager our best luck / on a dinosaur with a cotton
heart / as if for once / we both want the same thing: to touch
extinction / to see if it's loss / if it's kind

This brand new / desire: refashioning
childhood / from a less intimate ruin

If we could, we'd live forever / in arcade fluorescence / we'd live
forever in worship / of a neon god

Out in the familiar cold / we lift
our faces / for the moon to tiptoe on

Somewhere the war has begun / we don't hear
about it / though we feel the eloquence
of sulphur in our lungs

How lovely it is / you say / to have
a bed to forget yourself in / in a city
that doesn't love you

Key moans in the door lock / and we're back
at ground zero

Against the slow / pollen of pre-dawn
we unbutton our skin / to reveal the youngest
muscles in our bodies

Between our naked limbs / an almost blue immediacy
unfurls its petals

Blue Hour

Waves heave against fenced-in horizon.
They seek a listener, chime a single melancholy
note in the whorled ear
of a stranded shell, which I mistake

for your heartbeat. Where we live
sleep is expensive. But you purchase it
with your shallow breathing, cheek buried

in your pillow, and the moonlight
tonight is the lone traveller on the highway
of your spine. This is the blue hour

when all the music of the universe
is still waiting to be played
and everything is tinged with renewal exactly

the colour of a wintry sea. And the impossible
task of being wholly alone: the way

we once unbuttoned each other's skin,
our hands feverish with greed, right
down to the barest threads only

to find beneath it a circle
of friends & kin waiting
to glare at us, their inescapable eyes

wide with fear & suspicion.

How I long for the world to return
to its first form, a shoreless echo
like a foetal kick in ultrasound
strong as gold. Our bones

shall be folded back into star stuff, back
to their cosmic potential, all
phantom fires & radiant sawdust whizzing

through space, past the need for
speech towards
the same genesis. Instead,

the leaves in my head grow
too dense for thinking. They rustle
solemnly against life and yoke
pools of blue light as the bicycle

wheels in the trees
keep on spinning. Dawn breaks
against our skin, raw as a wound.

I watch the sheep stepping
gingerly out of the thick nets
of their own silhouettes

to tread the pebbles on the beach. Their faces
innocent & knowing as children's.

Convalescence

There is one species of woundedness
        I'd rather not be lifted from—
think hands cupped like a chalice
        just to hold the sting &
shimmer of seawater, then the hands
        slowly disappearing until
the water falls back into sea—
        because the pain, or what
initially felt like pain but turned out
        to be just shadows that grief
could cast, was unbearable, or simply
        because it was mine &
therefore harder to cast aside. *Enough*
        of this suffering, you buried her
with your own hands, remember how
        you tried to counsel me, being
the wiser of us two, as if words
        alone should suffice to put
an end to all that unravelling. Rescued
        or ruined, shattered or intact.
It hardly matters to anyone else now.
        Like what blurred by my window
this morning that I'd failed to save
        from the looming thunderstorm
(was it an oriole or saffron finch?)—what
        sought refuge from endless
wandering though I turned it away—I still

mourn, stroking the underwings
of a memory in whose fine details
of feathering I keep getting lost.
Then the skies clear, the fog finally lifting
like veils from the faces hidden
behind history. All that light, folding
and unfolding, like ceremonial robes.

Ode to My Uvula

No, it's not the damp star
of a uterus, nor the caramel
apple you swallowed many lives
ago. Remember, your uvula is the loudest
blossom on earth. When it's happy
it jiggles up & down like the rabbit's
fat pocket watch, though some
nights it's only a ragdoll that has drunk

a little too much, danced alone
to the wrong music and woken
in a ballroom full of strangers'
eyes. At home, your uvula
is a dagger shining with your
mother's blood. Its iron tongue
has stung the bosoms of those
you most love. Come winter

when all things wither, it will be
the sole eucalyptus tree
hanging from the sky's underbelly
where the shoreline meets
the woodland's jagged spine, the sun
bright as a polished crown. On the shore
a legion of men will pick up
fistfuls of mud

to pelt you with, & rocks to weigh
you down. But parting the waves
your uvula is a dead bird
rising from an oil spill off the farthest
coast, holding its scarlet
beak against the wind, fluttering
its red wings. No one can tell it
what songs to sing.

III Riverborne

Lullaby

of gloaming, of spring dirt, of rain
that we don't deserve
but falls anyway,

sing one for me though it's late
& the gods sleep in trees
with one eye open.

Sing one for me so I can climb
into its sonic garden
like a sprawling taproot

—gravity's favourite green baby
pulled back & slingshot
into pearlescent being.

My luck, big as a forest fire, rises
in woodsmoke from the altar
of my oil-slick throat

& thrusts into star-stitched sky
like a soaring church steeple,
my breath an unspooling

filigree of blue steam. Somewhere
a train wails. The whistle
burrows through night

like a cold bullet, bearing the news
of a death. *Hold me*, I say,
the way grief possesses a heart.

The way the dark cradles
a possum in its lulling arms.
Sing of a feathered love

so impossible to hurt
I'll want to stay
close & clear as thirst.

Self-Portrait as the Winter Sea

I thought I was the mirror
that could shelter lightning
beneath its skin. I was wrong: loveless,

fruitless, this season's music
is thrift. No more extravagant heaving
or unravelling as my waves lose the violence

of their original shape, as fish
hearts beating inside me mimic
stars' imperceptible fire.

I am the calm mind
of a philosopher—pure meditation hard
at work—a slow steel

gyroscope orbiting reason & logic. If
I had a body, it would know
the discipline of a Buddhist monk, what

it means to lay down all
that I am & become one with the sound
of the bell's tongue striking empty

space within. No wordsmith to take an axe
to my side & free frozen songs
from my chest. No captain to steer his ship

across me towards a dream of lilacs.
Season of gentle shores
& returning birds, be near, be near,

nearer still to my heart. Let me not be
a kingdom of sleep
& disappearance. But for each breath

I exhale, let it be a warm cave full
of prayers, a stage on which the world, waking,
rehearses its kindness.

Riverborne

were I to wake, ripple-cinched
        & desireless, among frost
    -bleached fleece of reeds

were I to rise, heat-swallowing, from the slip & spill
    of a billow through hush
                -enthroned rushes

while in the faltering light of a gesture

    or the unravelled bouquet of each echo

my unhitched spit of silt & pith rings true
        the way jostled cups of bone china do
    with their fluvial music of bone against bone

the way silence travels—neither as a mean chase
    of rose confetti nor
        a torn wreath of vying doves
    but as the banked snow of waves crashing

onto the foam-encrusted shore of
        the unsayable: fluid syllables of a heron's
    flight: the redness of a battle cry that wheels

like rain across the sky
as it wakes & wakes swift white wings

out of the bird's sun-loud soul

Telemachus Dreams of the Great Flood

If each dream is a thoroughbred, then
the mind is a poor stable to house such beasts.

In my dream, a great flood combs through the streets
like a fat tongue pushing through loose teeth.
On an uprooted red oak tree
two ravens plead, their hunger echoing & keen
as a cutlass.

A house buoyed by the flood
where a single lamp flickers like a gold wasp's
heart,
a man bending over the kitchen sink
rinses his kidney stones carefully
until each pain-pebble is smooth
as an eye's gelatinous lens.

He names them
after the Jovian moons: *Io, Callisto, Europa,*
voice brushing over the vowels like God running
a scabbed thumb-tip over the wind's dull blade
on the third day of creation.

In that dream, my father is the flood
sweeping through the neighbourhood.

But he's also the man bending over the sink
holding down the head of a beast—a horse,
a drunk god, a history—until its limbs
slacken like mooring ropes untied.

He watches water's strange navel, the sink
emptying itself in steady swirls
while, outside, flood plants the house
gently at a crossroad before it drains away.

Across the footpath, the oak lies flat & echoless.
My father dries his hands on his apron.
His hands are ravens.

Calligraphy Lesson

The sound of rain
outlives us.

—Li-Young Lee

What outlives even rain: the sound
of my father's ink settling like a final breath
onto rice paper's translucent skin.

Dark dew grazes the pink, creased ear
of an apple blossom. Of blossoms
or their proneness to bruise, I know

next to nothing. All I know is that
a whole forest tipped with frost
trembles inside as I apprentice myself

to the strength in my father's hand—
my small fist cradled in his
like a dirge caught in a swan's throat

& how the world unfurls in tendrils of fine
black silk between the flicks of our wrists, freed
from the tip of the horsehair brush:

天涯 *the sky's cliff edge* & 海角 *the sea's*
folded corner as if each stroke obliterates
a coast between us, distils a year still

to come. After the lesson, I lay the brush
gently against the gnarled forehead
of inkstone & turn to face my father

expecting, in innocence, the gift of a cool kiss
but he no longer recognises me.
He doesn't remember

that, in a past life, this ink we rinse
off the brush so freely now
was the blood that bound us together.

海, or Memory as a Water Language

At the beginning of every world: a yearning
like a twitching seed, awakening

into keen, green filigree. So it seems
I've dreamed of my own genesis

but it's only the sea's scent tugging
like a child's insistent fist at my breath's

tangled yarn. I feel the fresh salt stippling
my lungs crystalline—pink wings

wheezing as I test the shore. Bright veins
of geode gouge my soles. I think

of how 海, the Chinese word for *sea*,
depicts a mother with a sunhat, her face misted

by droplets of foam & spray. How memory—
of origin, of kinship—is always tethered

to water. Womb. Sky. A ribbon of sunset
purpling the known world's edge. How

my own mother, still alive, taught me to write
the sea in a language I've half-forgotten,

chalking strokes on a pebble she'd palmed
carefully to clear away the muck: 海.

A water language. A hidden wellspring
murmuring the first light into being.

It was as if she'd given the stone a tongue
to speak with, a poor muted thing licked smooth

& abandoned by waves. The train that took me
here to the sea's mouth has returned

to collect me. One remembers. One
forgets. The past never truly abandons us.

Grandfather Explains His Alzheimer's to Me

It's like boarding a slow-moving train
borne entirely on the wings of damselflies
and neither you nor the operator
knows where the train is headed.

Mangroves, or a Treatise on Ecological Inheritance

Faceless, of one mind, we have come
to know the depth of our own blood—

not the luxurious blue of sirens or
the lightning green of pond lilies, but brackish

as the spitting sea that will outlive us—ringing
ruthless shadows as desire rings the earth's

flesh. The heart is a long ladder, a mirrored
& sleeved thing. Our tongues have relished

the sweetness of this year's magnificence, our faith
lush & razor-edged. Out of the clear calm,

a shock of roots—hands of a virtuoso climb
& astonish. Here, in the north, our beauty

besieges winter. Men tread trees' memory
brazenly as tyrants do, not knowing the woodland

is our birthright, where the sun is all mouths
& the river writes her elegy on our limbs

tirelessly with her ink of light. Watch us toss
& lurch as a leafy coliseum under sky's

metallic sheen, each honest self burrowing deep,
staking a claim on what is ours to inherit.

Queer Physics: First Principle

Facts I'm relearning today: fear is red
like a warbler's throat. The moon
is only the sky's softest muscle.
Rusty & peeling as they are, the lacquered
horses of our childhood will outlast our bones
but not our songs. Not this one. The one
we sang in the back of a silver pick-up
until we began to float—our hearts all helium
in rubber skin. The one we sang to unfasten
the river from the boat we rowed into
a bloodshot sky, our lips knotted together
like balloon strings. Levitation is the first
principle of desire for boys who cling
to the flesh of other boys, believing love, like death,
empties the body into another. In the dream
where my limbs grow heavy as prayer, I sink
farther away from your hands & drown, song
turning to nacre on my tongue. Go ahead. Lift
the needle off the turntable. The dream
has stopped playing but I'm still singing.

Glass Boat, Glass Shore

Capitulation. Acts of salvage. Maple leaves, on the cusp
        of another flaming season, bow their heads reverently
as sudden drizzle descends to anoint their cheeks.

Where I once found sanctuary in the rock harbour
        that was his arm's crook—folds of skin redolent
of mock orange after rain & the not-yet-ripened

grip of desire—now neither of us can bear the nettle-sting
        of the other's touch. We let reticence bloom
wide as a year between us. Beneath our glass boat,

koi weave through water like silver shuttles through
        the fabric of a lucid dream & when we bend
over the gunwale to examine their translucent scales,

not once do they flinch from the cold blade of our fixed
        gaze. Simple trust. A kind of faith, whose purity
gets confounded with wilful blindness but, perhaps,

best resembles the near-silence of snow filling the spaces
        it sets out to fill—crevices, open crypts—as if
snow or silence had a mind of its own. And I find it

ever more difficult—though not yet impossible, not yet—
        to distinguish faith I never had from the faith I did
that has lost its lustre over the years. *Are houses burnt to ashes*

still homes? Can a single flake of ash bear the weight
of nostalgia? I ask the dusk gilding the shipwreck
of looming mountains as if it'd understand the kind

of belonging that lies at ruins' end. Above us the sea
of leaves swirls in gentle castigation. His hands,
which only last night had ebbed from the rough shore

of my skin, now frame my trembling waist. A quiet hum
pools in his mouth like moonlight in a varnished
chalice: a tentative minuet as I blur to bliss.

Under the maples searing towards a deeper shade
of crimson, two bodies sway and lift hymnward.
Leave them be. Leave their belief in forgiveness intact

and the stars over their heads
clear & quavering as tears.

Nocturne

This is the music of memory, water
entering the limbs, leaving lips echoless.
The room, unfurnished. A single dim light

dangles from the ceiling like a shadowy
fig. Years sifted clean in a stream
dividing the departed

from those who remain. Out
in the garden, the crescent moon hangs
its white fang on a branch. Someone, running,

always trips on the loose stone.
Another lets out a laugh the way
a glass bell shatters in anxious hands.

Look at us, each one
a shiny little impermanence
busy with our allotted task. We take turns

flipping over the hourglass. We carve
our names into the bare wall
& scrape them off with our fingertips.

Those who seek peace shall
have peace. Those who desire myths
shall have myths. Soon a small wave

will unclench its fist & give the storm
-tossed vessel back to the sand.
The untroubled blue

of the night sky will ink
through our skin. Tell me this
is how our flesh will be remembered.

IV At the Altar of Touch

Myth, or Luck as a Swan Boat

Fear fear, shriek the unseen cicadas in a borrowed
language all summer long. It forms a pattern:

the cut diamond of their chorus shredding air
into thin ribbons of heat. An abandoned fountain

dry as the loins of any stone cherub. I go where
chance takes me, or is it luck—that sun-bleached

swan boat steered by nothing but the lake's caprice
through the knot of shadows cast by a willow grove.

That shadow play of *mind : foliage : mind : foliage*
until the water turns murky as unanswered prayers—

chance, a codeword for surrender; prayers, a prelude
to trust. I lie down beside the rock worn to myth

by the lake's ancient murmurs. The boat I came in
has turned to a swan, the swan now saunters towards me

as a god. Fear ebbs from me in ripples tainted by the moon
as I seek that rare kind of tenderness that lies between *rescue*

and *ruin*, guiding the god's feathered touch over the ivory
magnolia of my belly, steering his calloused hands over

mine, saying, *Here are the oars. Here is the impossible rowing.*

At the Altar of Touch

I.
Exiled from his homeland
by war, Xu Beihong painted horses
from memories of a bucolic childhood.

As Japanese soldiers thrust bayonets
into Chinese bellies—flesh riddled
with new eyes that opened, unseeing,

into blood—the artist picked up
his paintbrush to transmute paper
into breath: caught in a gallop, hooves

suspended in the air like upended
wedding bells, neck tensed & shiny
as the sinewed back of a waterfall, the beast

is an ink-wash tincture of stillness
& perpetual motion, its mane lifted
not by wind itself

but by the suggestion of a wind
that is the absence of ink, a silence
echoing like the deep sighs of leaves.

II.
I kneel in the night boat under
the soft machinery of the dark,

choking on the blue threads
of hymns I try to exorcise

from my throat. The fish pause
in their flight through water to watch

my undoing—expectant little
faces, thimble-mouths widening

into soundless cries of bubbles.
I cough & gag & out comes the pale

-green jade that was once sewn
into the seam of my grandma's

cheongsam by her ailing mother
the night the train took her

away from the war. But before
the farewell, a few words

of caution: *Be careful what*
you worship with your hands.

The night is always watching
even when it isn't.

III.
Having wakened from the death
-stupor of an afternoon nap,

my father plays Rachmaninoff's
Piano Concerto No. 2 on a battered

turntable, eyes shut—as if snowblind—
against a sunset sombre as nostalgia,

crimson as dove's blood. As the strings
swell & crash onto the shore of his life,

he raises his hands & marshals the air
the way a memoirist weaves memories

into history. Outside: the loud applause
of gunshots & the distant droning of metal

hearts as planes lance through the clouds.
It's the anniversary of the founding of

the Republic. My father mourns the death
of his childhood, the receding calm

of those mountains he scaled barefoot
in winter, too poor to afford the luxury

of warmth. When he opens his eyes again
& reads the bewilderment in my face, he

wipes his cheek with the heel of his palm
& says, *I'm turning chaos into order!*

IV.

Walk with me, says Xu Beihong
so we step inside his painting
& stroll to the edge of the faintly

painted field, where a few dashes of sun
-beaten reeds sway in unison
& the horses are drinking straight

from the source of the artist's
sorrow, muzzles glistening
with small quivering pearls

of water. *Speak to them*
with your hands, he instructs patiently
as he steers my fingers slowly

from a chestnut's sweat-mottled
withers to the taut skin of its back
as if showing a blind boy the body

of a violin for the first time, how
he could awaken the strings
with his touch &, by awakening

the strings, touch a deep chord
within himself. And I can finally see
with my hands that the horse's body

is tense with listening & obedience,
that these are no horses
at all but souls.

V.

Lying still as a whisper in the dark
& exiled from sleep, Rachmaninoff
strokes his own face as though

it were the skin of a long dead lover,
as though it were the snow-draped
landscape of Russia before the Bolsheviks.

Across the room, the piano stands lonely
& griefless as a glacier, frigid from neglect.
The Californian moon runs across the keys

like a long scar. Then the dream returns,
slowly, but more vivid than ever: February,
Moscow, through emaciated birch trees,

the growling thunder of hoofbeats.

VI.
On the lawn chair
in the windmilling sun
Grandmother has drifted to sleep,

her thumb armoured
in a thimble—the only relic
of atrocities. A little breeze pecks

at her half-embroidered silk.
Her needle slips
from between her fingertips

like a silver tear into the long grass
as if the old world of suffering
has dropped away, all of it

an elaborate falsehood
from the well-thumbed book
of her mind. No recollection

of a weeping mother or fields
sown with unburied bones.
Above her, the maple blazes & shivers

like a defoliating dream. In the distance
a train announces itself
in the language of smoke.

Meadow

In my body's rain-scented cavern, night loosens
its mouth's well-oiled hinge. The man who dived deep
beneath my skin & emptied out his sudden pearls
now lies shipwrecked & desireless beside me, silence
between our bodies a meadow I can't bring myself
to cross. O wind-twisted magnolia, who diligently
paved my window with sweetness all summer, teach me
how to be marked by faith without being
swallowed by its light. I should confess that when he came
inside me like the softest knife I've ever felt, all I could
think of was my mother's throat lit by the thistle
moon's white fire years ago—as she tied around her cool flesh
a necklace strung with the pointed bullets
she'd picked from my father's drawer, when
the field outside bristled with anticipation
of autumn (though it was not yet the end of summer,
no, not yet) & it was still easy to believe that the blue flame
of the cicadas' song among the high leaves
would go on & on.

Peacock

So much love, and it can do nothing against death!
—César Vallejo

It lies by the motorway's rain-shrouded
shoulder, motionless & mud-robed. Orphaned
        by the morning sky's sparsely starred veil.

An overlooked martyrdom of bloodied
plumes. Green sail, unfurled, of a thousand
        wild eyes: some wide as if stunned

by a clean death's swiftness, others
half-shut, exhausted by the afterlife
        or else lamenting its emptiness, yet

each one still glistening turquoise under
the featherweight mirror of a raindrop—
        feathered eyes still swaying the way a clique

of crocuses leans into the wind's tuneless
dirge, impaling their throats on the pale
        let-down branches of sun. Birdsong

made sweeter by the birds' silence. Rain
made more eloquent by its own absence
        & narrow sky clear as a strip of sheer

blue gauze. I stand in the not-song
& not-rain and weep in open daylight.
        I weep for a loss though many would say

it's no loss at all. *It was an accident. The bird*
deserved it for its sin of pride. You should save
        your grief for the humbled dead ones,

like the swan frozen by the pond or
the dove cut down by a child's slingshot.
        So what's the harm then? Why grief

like a hidden deer leaping straight
from the heart's fountain? Still
        I weep and no one, not even the river

that turns back in its sun-streaked longing,
understands my tears' limpid
        ceremony. No one understands the dirt hill's

loneliness except the hill itself—who
loved the arrogant peacock with the secrecy
        & devotion of a trailing shadow, who loved

and admired the silly bird in flight even
though it chased and loved another
        of its own kind. It seems I weep for a love

even I myself do not understand. My grief
is nothing compared to the hill's, whose love
        will remain alive in the gleaming of every

leaf & silence of every stone. So much
love, and still, it can do nothing against
        death. Still, the bird does not rise. It lies

with its head buried in the creased heap
of mud like a bride slumped over her beloved's
        grave, having cried herself to sleep

and would not wake until the dead rose
from the grave, shiny & whole as a prophecy
        fulfilled. Just imagine the rain returning

with its handful of harp strings, shivering
into a joyous glissando: a blessing for the raising
        & the reunion. So, my bride. My martyr.

My miracle-worker. My sole consolation
amid the listless indifference of the world.
        Rise now. Cast off the grey net of your sleep

the way I'm learning to scour the work of
sorrow off my cheeks—my heart entombed in
        the lush foliage of your plumes as I try, in vain,

to roll away these unwanted pearls.

Here Again, Yet the Day

lengthens like smoke / like the spine
of the shadow cat with one crooked leg / scratching
its way up the chimney

Boys with moon-bruised shoulders / we chase
our own hands / from dawn to dusk

Remember when the days / were all
sequined / Remember when / the trees in my eyes
grew so tall they could touch the cloud

Why don't we sit / on the cooling edge
of this quiet alive / our lives scattered around us
like loose change

Admit that it's enough for now / to watch lights
eat the city / one street at a time / to watch
here-before / shift from bloodberry
to blue swarms

I watch you reach for your word / like an invisible
sword / while all night / rain pains the window

A koi windsock ripples / into the wind's
silver mouth / We dream of waking
under each other's skin / my sweat

on your tongue like a world
of pearls / There's no loneliness
like ours

Requiem with a Singing Kimono

Our entire spoken life is one long sentence ...

—Mary Ruefle

I.

So we find ourselves at the ends
of our sentences, my mother & I.
I, an old man, hair thinned to a pale
wreath of frozen steam, while
she, still thirty-six & delicate
as a whisper, having never aged
a day from the morning she died.
Gently, I carry her on my back
like the daughter I never had
as we track the palimpsestic
hoofprints in a snow-effaced field.
From the sun's blind eye
blazing in sky
time falls, soundless, like ash or
a hymn of ground glass. *Where*
are we going? She
never asks. Such is her trust
in my judgement, even
at the intersecting ends
of our lives. I feel a shiver flashing
through the frail whisper
of her body and I
am afraid.

II.

Of losing her, I was
not prepared. How to steady
oneself against loss when
the losing never ends.
Yet there she was
in the pristine snowdrift
of her hospital bed—delirious
as a feverish child in the throes
of her death, and in the sheer
exhaustion of dying
she turned to me slowly
as if to say something (perhaps
she wanted a final word
or just a last sip of water).
Then the saying faltered.
Her sentence, unfinished.
Something inside me found
its release like the vision
of a falcon freed from
its blinder. Through the open
window, a wood thrush trills
a clear flute note. Outside,
summer has just begun.

III.

The sentence you wanted to finish
never finishes.
You, who never meant
to leave, are leaving.

IV.
Drifting
like immaculate scales
carefully stripped off the back
of a silver koi, the snow
continues to fall. It sings
as it falls. It sings not like a songstress
but like the kimono she wears
as her skin catches fire
from the spotlight.
A singing kimono, shredded
to a handful of notes.
That song: the cold
scent of time. *Put me down, my*
child, my mother begs me
just when I thought she'd fallen
asleep.

V.
Put me down
so alone you can still make it.
But where is it I'm headed
when you are no longer here
to make it with me. Even
in this dream I have of our fleeting
reunion, the guilt of dying
has made you delirious again.
You should know you were never
the burden. You're every journey
I take without knowing.

Without you, the road disappears
beneath me. Without you, of whose
unfinished sentence
do I sing?

Lullaby

Before the divine invention of dawn
          & grief, before all bare
beginnings, is the body's intention

          to sing. The river wants to hear it
& so do shadows abandoned
          by their owners under the chestnut tree,

waiting with their palms extended
          as if in supplication
like the vagrant in Bruegel's painting.

          Here in the garden, time waits
like the slowest fire while
          autumn dies in eddies of clear amber.

Having planted my voice here
          in the garden by spring's
end—where I've prayed for harvest

          but the soil remains stubbornly
fruitless, I can no longer sing
          yet the night air parts before me

of its own accord as water cleaved
          by vibration & through its sheer blue
curtains drifting apart, I can make out

snow geese lifting the cold songs
of their bodies—unimpeded by
hunger, nor by their dresses of damp

feathers—towards a light
we on earth no longer believe in.

Opera

Listen, you say to the salmon-pink horizon
waking from its dream
of a different silence, even though

you don't know how the world has aged
so steadily into ruin
or how to save it from its own hands, only

that this hour wears the morning song
of cockatoos like a rhinestone choker
around its pale throat.

Sunlight branches into your room
like a tree of amber & your body is a book
of prayers that's only been opened once.

Listen, even as your father sings on the balcony
to his own reflection in a handheld mirror
he demands the sun's

attention: *Snip Snip* with his lightning blade
as hair falls from his pitted chin
into the plastic wash basin like dark pollen.

Peking Opera swims through his chest, slick
as a silver fish & when he reaches the part
where the old king, betrayed by all

but one, bids farewell to his faithful beloved, his voice
trembles like the hand of a stable boy
combing through a foal's grass-soft mane.

Then he can no longer bear the weight
of his own song, which is exactly
the weight of living however you look at it,

for this loss is absolute. This horizon dreaming
the same silence. This mirror in your father's
hand, a tilted ache—the one light

he can't turn his eyes from. You rise
out of your shadow & take it from his hand
like a kingdom you're waiting to inherit.

V The Resurrection

Dreaming Mask

'Death, being the inexorable fate
of all men, is either lighter
than the feather of a wild goose

or heavier than Mount Tai,' writes
Sima Qian, as though death is nothing
if not beautiful: the soul falling—in a brief

trance-like dance—from the tree of time
like a wilting dream of a leaf, or arching
against history, majestic & snow-peaked.

But today, in Yemen, death is the swift kiss
of a bullet on a child's cheek, the indifferent
hand of the wind shoving sand into open

graves, is nothing more than the dust
-mantled face of a seven-year-old boy
carried in the bruised arms of a war-

wearied father, captured & frozen
in time by the cold eye of an American lens.
Except for dust & a streak of dried blood,

the child's face was so lifelike & peaceful
you'd almost mistake death
for a mask that life wears in its dreaming.

And behind his dreaming face, stillness falls
like centuries of snow through which
his father will trudge, as a pilgrim staggering

towards a shrine, to unbury his small body
again & again—lifting it limb by limb
from the ruins that had crushed his skull, which

his father cradles in his lap—a lantern made holy
by its brokenness—rocking back
& forth, humming a little, dirt-cracked lips perfumed

with a lullaby as he wipes the blood
& dust off his son's face. *Death is either lighter*
than the feather of a wild goose or heavier

than Mount Tai. Indeed, nothing is lighter
than the death of a boy fallen on the sword-edge
of a war: not feathers nor leaves nor the dream

of snow drifting onto the battlefield
& ice sheathing the grass billowing like a sea
of green candle flames around the boy's

grave, a tiny mountain in the desert, which
is heavy—but not so heavy as his death—
& just as snowbound as the red tent

of his father's heart.

Needle

She threw up again, my father's muffled voice
eels through the receiver two shores away, & all

I can hear is worry whetting its tapered blade
on the stone at the bottom of his throat.

I imagine him home, brows glazed with sweat
from work, pushing his body a little further through

the day like a blunt needle—all his fifty-five years
trailing behind him like thick threads too matted

to unravel—& my baby sister, slung over his
shoulder, weak-limbed as a newborn horse, still drunk

on the sorrow over her own body's betrayal, puffy eyes
squandering generous drops of opal onto his shirted back.

Once, this was me: a small, ruminant mammal
spilling every world it'd swallowed through the haunted

doorway of its missing teeth, coughing up
an anthill, a bird nest, or a swarm of jewelled wasps,

and still, my father would hold me to his chest
closer than breath. Still, he'd pat my back until

the last Atlas moth crawled out from my mouth's
corner. Tonight, the stars hang low & sparse

at his window. Night drips into the house
like a rusting spigot. In the chiaroscuro

of the dining room, he crouches to scrape away
the putrid scraps with a dishcloth, his knees'

brittle saucers pressed dangerously
to the tiled floor. Boil-scarred & graceless, his hand arcs

across slabs of black granite, redrafting the evening
as the words he meant to utter sink deeper

into his throat. Untold nights like this
on which my father loses count

of himself, scouring off the soot & grime
so that our faces may shine.

'Can Dyslexics Read? Can You Prove it?'

queried the boy who plopped himself down
on the seat before me, two burly
accomplices flanking my desk
to kill any impulse for an early exit.
He'd carefully selected my demise
for that day, opened my textbook
to the Wordsworth poem
Ms. L wanted us to recite, his eyes
sharpened by curiosity's
violent light, the kind that drives boys,
otherwise innocent, to shoot & flay
sparrows in the terrible noon
heat, fingers twisting bloody
in the miniature labyrinths
of exposed innards. My mind
the flayed sparrow wishing
for flight. My mind an apparition
roaming the smoke-choked hall
of the Roman alphabet, each letter
a cracked mirror in which another
might appear, perfectly twinned.
Each day, I woke to my tongue
heavy with the burden of unhindered
utterance, a pink muscle
waiting for fluency—
consonants all barbed, vowels
singeing the inside of my mouth

like branding irons I wished
I could swallow. Later, when I asked
Ms L if she could help me
with the recitation, help me
make Wordsworth less cruel
on my tongue—my face still burning
with the silver hooks of tears—
all she taught me was a simple
melody. *Sing out the words*
though tuneless the singing might be.
Let it trickle clear & slow through the lips
until the clouds stopped ticking
like vaporous bombs & the daffodils
all sheathed their tiger-teeth
while all this time, she held my upturned
palms so that I didn't have to wander
lonely through the song.

Falling

I was thinking, how, despite years of dogged
        practice, English is still the slick
winged serpent the dull flute of my tongue

has failed to charm: cracked syllables slithering
        past a rein of pink muscle
into audible exoticness that marks me as alien

on this side of the planet. How I envy you native
        speakers—your minds falling
into the language like agile skinny-dippers diving

straight through water, your mind-bodies unimpeded
        by the gravity of syntax.
When you mean to say you're in or out of love

the verb is almost always *fall*, not *plunge* or *parachute*,
        never *bellyflop*. How I wanted
to invent my own physics of English! Still, at school,

I fell prey to shame like a day-old lamb caught
        in a lion's mouth. Wishing
all my vowels would be rinsed clean of their knotted

foreignness, I whip-trained my wild tongue until it fell
        in line with every phonetic rule.
When the boy I'd loved in bashful secrecy finally touched

me & touched me & touched me until my body
 was a high bright whistle, I thought
This must be what it means, in English, to fall—eyes closed,

trusting the air to hold you as if it were your own
 flesh. Not the way Icarus fell—mid
-flight, mouth agape, betrayed by sun's searing heat

as wax-tipped feathers streamed from his back
 like jet plane contrails. But the way
dusk once fell across pebbled path, shaded by curlicues

of azalea blooms, as I walked home each afternoon years
 ago, repeating out loud the day's lesson:
The rain in Spain falls mainly in the plain, so I could dream

at night of freefalling off my tongue's steep cliff through
 perfect English & still, each morning,
I'd rise faithfully from death.

The Resurrection

Ashes in November. & the fanatic
burgeoning of a bushfire, the hush afterwards
clean as amnesia—its onslaught
demarcated by retreating birdcall.
Each spring, through the changing light of the valley, there
falls wondrous rain. Green gowns strew
gnarled roots, sewn with sprigs of
holly. Seen from a reverent distance, smoke
issues from a rustic cottage
jagged as a jilted bride's torn veil. Over the bald
knoll, a choir of clouds uncoils
like rumours passed between tongues. In devastations like this,
memory becomes aftermath. Soft-bellied sun
nuzzles lush summer sleeves of the resurrected
oak. Imagine the intimacy of two
people lying under this oak, wearing nothing but
quivers. Such trust. They must've bathed in the same
river, long before the quieter one
said anything to the other, before they even
touched what must've been forbidden to them. Autumn
ushers in undeserved grace: wings returning briefly to the
v-trees, crowns of berry-strung branches & familiar
warbles. The earth forgets nothing. To gather
xenoliths after the test of lava, to
yearn as leaves do, stirred by a swell of
zephyr. May the fire teach us.

Alyssum, Honed

The dream where your mother made you practise
the oboe all winter until your blood hymned *mercy*
was the one in which you learned to disown
the snow. Sure, this was years after the burial. Long
after that whisper in the dark had unlaced her body
like gauze, and you'd swallowed every mirror in town
just to feel clarity like music through your bones. But imagine,
for a moment, the sorrow of salt. Its papery flutter against
the tip of your nose like the embers of a long-forgotten
song. The one your mother hummed as she drew
from her throat's soft cave the thin shard of glass
she'd honed her voice on. Imagine snow in her arms
like a bouquet of sweet alyssum as she walked down
to the water. Imagine her freedom when the river—quivering
silver under the moon's lips—stepped inside her, too.

Your Gratitude

It is the fragrance of a cake of soap
        the pregnant duchess, plump
            -bellied, emerging from a bath, steps on
before tumbling to a puddle of starry oblivion.

It is a parade of blindfolded children shoving a grand piano
        built from exhaustion & laughter
happily down the shadowy slope of a hill, the sun warm
        & glittery on bare arms.

It is the woman wearing a choker of meteors standing
        at the centre of your mind's
amphitheatre, singing for decades the same aria

while buzzards converge before her on the acacia
branches, above
the rotting carcass of a wild hart
waiting to be picked apart,

& the plate of wolfberries
on your table bearing the glad
faces of the deceased
desert travellers, lips still praying
for the promised rain.

& the arms of your father cradling you
on your first day here.

Long before candlelight
& joyrides, God had invented
tears in his eyes. Such

astonishing brightness
in the eyes of a mortal! As though—

as though
the railings of his cradle
could be made from something
soft as ether, clear as dew.

'COVID'

mutters the white man in the whole
-food aisle: cue his scratched-vinyl
voice: cue the leering skull
inked on his arm staring straight
out of two blackholes
through your yellow-peril soul
and you're the devil who's out spreading
his sick of sin in this cut-paper town tonight.

Go home and die, you dirty chink. An extra dose
of reassurance just in case you haven't heard
enough. What's not to love? This
outlaw country that wants you dead each day
but not dead enough to be absolved
of your crime of still breathing
& trying to cling to the incandescent
cadence of your heart.

In the floodlit church
of the supermarket, on this dog-eared
& rain-beaten evening, you stand aflame
like an origin story no one wants
to hear, a chink in the chainmail armour
of a history shining with the fiery
scherzo of poppies & gold-plaqued names
of colonial heroes. You touch the blue

plastic bag of long-grained rice
and think of terraced paddies in Sichuan
gleaming with their silver tresses
of ripening seeds that thrash in the sun
like your grandmother's plaited hair. A lineage
braided & unbraided. You stroke the green corsage
of a bok choy and think of kin, of

blood history, of how the skein of vein throbbed
under Grandma's wrist like a slight, fearless
tremor of earth. 'Covid-19 China Die' was
spray-painted on the garage door of one
Chinese family in Victoria.

What's not to love here?
One yellow body = an entire land
of brown earth where the wind lingers
in fine strokes of hieroglyphs and the swaying
bamboo stalks talk in pentatonic
scales of flute & zither.

And the rumour they've heard is all
true: you breathe through your chink-in-the-wall
your chink-in-the-curtain mouth
and out comes the rice-paper moon
Li Bo wrote about as he lay among
a bed of peonies fifteen centuries ago, drunk
on sweet plum wine & the old grief
of unassuageable loss.

And you alone tonight are China
gleaming with harvest. You, alone, are Li Bo
drunk on grief. You alone are the Chinese moon
drifting through aisles promising
deliverance & plenitude
lifting the light pouring from above
to your burning lips
and you drink.

A Chord of Light

Fields of barley recede in the rear-view mirror
        like honey sucked through a straw. Suddenly
you're back in the body of your newborn self

when everything your heart touched spoke with
        the tongue of rain, back in your father's beat-up
black sedan—which he drives exactly at the speed

of his thought that darts between the reaches of
        clouds above & the gravel road ahead the way
a hummingbird composes the air's stillness

as it flits from one sprig of heliotrope to the next—
        & back in your mother's arms as she sleeps,
her head against the car window's one-way mirror,

while the sun brushes crushed pollen of its aria
        across her cheeks without tearing a single
ripple in the lake-surface of her dream, & how memory

undresses flesh the way dawn picks with great care
        the ink-washed petals off every shadow, how
it is her dreaming that's made the road, clouds

& fields real, real as the softness of your newborn flesh
        that houses the soul of a rain-struck lily, real
as the chord of light driven like a sliver of isinglass

into the heart of your palm each time you raise it
        to ward off arrows of the sun's music—which
marks you without wounding you, bewilders you without

leading you astray, so you'd feel saved at the road's
        end where nothing else in the world would
spare you—to remind you this is the body

you will always return to.

Wild Nothing

On winter nights like this when my chest
aches for the wild nothing hiding its face

in the frost-trimmed dark, the older man
I used to love more than any real danger

must be sitting alone in the ceramic boat
of his bathtub with an empty glass in hand

in an empty glass town five state lines away,
all wined up & soap-warm. If his hands, strong

as a seagull's neck, had once taught me how
to rein in the affection of a proud horse,

how to triumph over the headwind
on horseback as the world around me

flakes off in bright lines—they'd also taught
my body to fizzle & froth into birdsong. I want

to call him up at once & lay bare all
the joy & loss I've locked away

then I remember I haven't called in years.
Not since the night he banished me from

his house & must've rushed out the door
afterwards, trailing the wake of my shadow

like a shark adrift in strange waters, searching
for me at the roadside café where we once hid

from a hailstorm & talked breathlessly for hours
about plans for a future we've both slipped off.

I imagine him leaning back against the tub
tonight, no longer regal, bruising the air

with wreaths of smoke exhaled from a mouth
creased by age, as embers fall from the dying

sun of his cigarette onto cooling bathwater
the way all memories & laughter eventually

turn to ash, & somewhere in Idaho, the horse
we once rode has grown old, its ragged breath

warm & moist as a hothouse rose in the icy cell
of its barn stall. I listen to telephone wires

trill like a field of cricket noise above
the battered neon sign of the all-night deli

& I burn for what's no longer mine.

Requiem Ending with the Night Sky

Lilac sings in the bridal shower of the wind: bells
of purple, now brightening to indigo, chiming
quicksilver in the changing autumn light
like a children's choir. Children fall
as petals, forgotten by all

but the earth. The ghosts of their voices
graze like lambs in the dead's
pasture, content with their share
of green & sun. Or not-green
& not-sun, for it's long past midnight here

on earth, past the hour of abundance
marked by the lamb-sweet innocence of longing
& letting go. I thought if I lived long
enough, I'd forgive myself for failing to become
inured to suffering; I'd forgive myself

for living, always greedy for more. Clouds
bank up over a crush of clovers. My dead
gather around me year after year.
Still, the letting-go gets no easier. The grass
spills beneath me to reveal a path

of gaunt green shadows. The similes
halt in their ploughed trails. Above me
the night sky is necklaced with the bright murmuring
of deathless stars. Their hopes & sorrows
are mine & immortal.

Notes

'Distant Hills' alludes to the origin story of 'the passion of the cut sleeve', a Chinese idiom used to describe homosexual desire. The story goes that one afternoon when rising from his bed from a nap, Emperor Ai of Han, in trying to avoid waking his courtier and lover Dong Xian, cut off his own shirt sleeve that his lover was sleeping on.

The 'Abing poems' are based on the life of the blind Chinese folk musician Hua Yanjun (1893–1950), better known as Abing, famed for his erhu compositions and performances. He lived a vagrant life during the years of Japanese Invasion of China. His most famous composition is entitled *Erquan Yingyue* (二泉映月), meaning 'The Moon's Reflection on the Second Spring'.

'Self-Portrait as the Winter Sea': The lines, 'No wordsmith to take an axe/ to my side & free frozen songs / from my chest' are inspired by Franz Kafka's letter, dated 27 January, 1904, to his childhood friend, Oskar Pollak, in which Kafka writes: 'A book must be the axe for the frozen sea inside us.'

'Calligraphy Lesson': The epigraph is excerpted from Li-Young Lee's poem 'Water' in *Rose*, BOA Editions, Ltd., New York, 1986.

'Nocturne': The line, 'This is the music of memory, water' is from Derek Walcott's poem 'The Prodigal' in *The Prodigal: A Poem*, Farrar, Straus and Giroux, New York, 2004.

'At the Altar of Touch': The line, 'the soft machinery of the dark' is from Jack Gilbert's poem 'Going Wrong' in *The Great Fires*, Alfred A. Knopf, Inc., New York, 1994. Sections of the poetic sequence are inspired by the life and art of the Chinese painter, Xu Beihong (1895–1953), primarily known for his ink paintings of horses and birds. The two paintings alluded to in Sections I and IV are *Galloping Horse* and *Horses Drinking*, the former of which I first saw on the front cover of my Year 7 Chinese Literature textbook. Xu Beihong painted *Galloping Horse* in the autumn of 1941 while holding exhibitions in Penang, Malaysia, where he received news from home that the Imperial Japanese Army had recently invaded and massacred the City of Changsha in Southern China. Section II of the sequence is based on my paternal grandmother's account of her experience fleeing her hometown during the Japanese Invasion.

'Peacock': The epigraph is excerpted from Robert Bly's English translation of César Vallejo's poem 'Masses' in *Neruda and Vallejo: Selected Poems*, Beacon Press, Boston, 1971. 'So much/ love, and still, it can do nothing against/ death' is a slight variation of the epigraph.

'Requiem with a Singing Kimono': The epigraph is from Mary Ruefle's interview with Tony Leuzzi, entitled 'The Life-Long Sentence' in *The Brooklyn Rail*, New York, July–August 2014.

'Lullaby': In the line, 'Before the divine invention …' the painting referenced in this poem is Pieter Bruegel the Elder's

The Census at Bethlehem, 1566, Royal Museums of Fine Arts of Belgium, Brussels.

'Dreaming Mask': The poem begins with my own translation of a quote from 'Letter to Ren An' by the Chinese historian, Sima Qian (139–86 BC), who is considered a pioneer of Chinese historiography for his *Records of the Grand Historian*, a general history of Ancient China covering more than two thousand years. The original quote in Chinese is '人固有一死, 或重于泰山, 或轻于鸿毛'.

'Falling': The line '*The rain in Spain falls mainly in the plain*' is a slight variation of 'the rain in Spain stays mainly in the plain' from the song 'The Rain in Spain' (lyrics by Alan Jay Lerner) from the musical *My Fair Lady*.

'COVID': The line, 'Covid-19 China Die' refers to the content of a racist graffiti spray-painted by vandals on the garage door of a Chinese-Australian family's home in Melbourne, Victoria on 20 April 2020.

Acknowledgements

Most of the poems in this manuscript were written on the lands of the Turrbal people so I want to express my sincerest gratitude to their Elders. I would also like to give thanks to the editors of the following publications, in which some of these poems here or their earlier incarnations were first published: *Atticus Review*, *Australian Poetry Journal*, *Cordite Poetry Review*, *Dunes Review*, *Entropy*, *Everything, All At Once* (Ultimo Press, 2021), *Foundry*, *Glass: A Journal of Poetry*, *Hobart* (USA), *HOUSEGUEST*, *Inscape Journal*, *Meanjin*, *Nashville Review*, *New England Review*, *Parentheses Journal*, *Peril Magazine*, *Plumwood Mountain*, *Poet Lore*, *Rabbit Poetry Journal*, *Ruminate Magazine*, *Stilts*, *StylusLit*, *Sundog Lit*, *The Boiler Journal*, *The Cincinnati Review*, *The Journal* (Ohio State University), *The Oleander Review*, *The Southampton Review*, *Tinderbox Poetry Journal*, *Up the Staircase Quarterly*, *Voice & Verse Poetry Magazine* (Hong Kong), *Voiceworks*, *Waxwing* and *Wildness*.

Immeasurable gratitude to my editor Felicity Plunkett for her endless patience, kindness and resourcefulness and for believing in this book even when I felt I was at my wits' end.

Deep gratitude to my teachers for their generosity, wisdom and inspiring examples of craftsmanship, especially Russell Brakefield, Tarfia Faizullah, Linda Gregerson, Laura Kasischke, Megan Levad, Keith Taylor, Cody Walker and John Whittier-Ferguson.

Thank you to my friends for their friendship and love and for being a shoulder to cry on in difficult times, especially Hailey Bonner, Peggy Chang, Fenghua Chen, Zenobia Frost, Grey Grant, Maggie Yi Guo, Kathy Hua, Anna Jacobson, Edward Lai, Emily Mei, Bryan Shaofeng Shu and Wenyi Zhou.

To my dear friend and brother in poetry Will Georges, I will always cherish our friendship and time together.

I want to thank my grandparents, Dingzhong Yuan and Jinfeng Lei, for raising me when their daughter couldn't. I owe everything in my life to them. I would also like to acknowledge my father, Xuwen Gao, who was the first reader of everything I wrote as a child and planted in me the precious seed of poetic sensibility.

Finally, to my mother, who took me to art classes every Saturday morning when I was four and with frustration and amusement watched me disobey every rule noted by the teacher with my paintbrush, this book is about you, inspired by you and for you. Thank you for watching over me. You are never absent from my life. You are behind every poem I write.